HOW (NOT) TO READ THE BIBLE

Making Sense of the
**ANTI-WOMEN, ANTI-SCIENCE,
PRO-VIOLENCE, PRO-SLAVERY,**
and Other Crazy-Sounding
Parts of Scripture

STUDY GUIDE | SIX SESSIONS

DAN KIMBALL

H Harper*Christian*
Resources

How (Not) to Read the Bible Study Guide
© 2021 by Dan Kimball

Requests for information should be addressed to:
HarperChristian Resources, 3900 Sparks Dr. SE, Grand Rapids, Michigan 49546

ISBN 978-0-310-14861-6 (softcover)
ISBN 978-0-310-14862-3 (ebook)

HarperChristian Resources titles may be purchased in bulk for church, business, fundraising, or ministry use. For information, please e-mail ResourceSpecialist@ ChurchSource.com.

Cover design: Darren Welch Design
Cover images: © iStock
Interior design: Denise Froehlich and Kait Lamphere

First Printing October 2021 / Printed in the United States of America

Contents

Introduction v
How to Use This Guide. vii

Session 1: Never Read a Bible Verse (Or You Will Have to Believe
in Magical Unicorns). 1
Session 2: Stranger Things: Shrimp, Slavery, and Skin of a Dead Pig . . . 21
Session 3: Boys' Club Christianity: Is the Bible Anti-Women?. 41
Session 4: Jesus Riding a Dinosaur: Is the Bible Anti-Science?. 63
Session 5: My God Can Beat Up Your God: Does Christianity
Claim All Other Religions Are Wrong? 83
Session 6: Rated NC-17: The Horror of Old Testament Violence 103

Closing Words. 122
Leader's Guide 125

Introduction

Welcome to *How (Not) to Read the Bible*. This guide, including six teaching sessions, is meant to be a companion learning experience to my book, *How (Not) to Read the Bible*. And here's why this study is so important. The Bible has become a stumbling block for many Christians and non-Christians alike. The strange and disturbing verses we read prevent many of us from taking the Bible seriously, not to mention the memes we see about these verses. I can totally relate to anyone who thinks the Bible is strange. I did too. In fact, that's why I'm here.

Maybe you're here because you are a Christian and you find yourself uncomfortable with your growing awareness of Bible verses and stories you never paid much attention to before. Or maybe you're here because you have a friend or family member doubting and even deconstructing their faith, and you're hoping for insight or a way to respond. And maybe you're here because you're starting to explore Jesus' teachings, what the Bible says, and what it means to be a Christian.

Whatever your reason for being here, this study experience is meant to be your guide for understanding the validity of the Bible. We live in a day and age when there are many sacred religious books out there, when people are asking how we know if the Bible is *the one* sacred text for our lives, a revelation from God. And who's to say the Bible and its teachings make sense for us today? We can no longer just sweep these questions under the rug and ignore them without taking a look at the origins of the Bible. This is the only way to understand the bizarre and unusual things in it.

Although you may not know me personally, I can say this very confidently to you: *I would not be teaching this study experience if there were no explanations for these verses in the Bible.* And I would never mislead anyone into believing in a faith that is not trustworthy. The good news is we can intelligently, with faith, believe that the Scriptures are from God. While there are many verses that seem difficult to comprehend, we can find legitimate responses for these bizarre Bible verses and difficult questions when we apply certain study methods and examine these verses in their contexts. Understanding how *not* to read the Bible changes how we view and read it every day.

So, here's where we're heading over the next six sessions. First, we'll learn what to do when we come across crazy-sounding Bible passages. Second, we'll look at several of the passages most commonly objected to. And we'll look at five areas of challenge to the Bible and ways to address those challenges. While there are plenty more strange and confusing Bible passages we could cover, these five give us a helpful place to start. Together, we will look at how to find intelligent responses for these challenging passages so that you have the basic methods to keep exploring in the future.

Let's get started!

Dan Kimball, www.dankimball.com

How to Use This Guide

How *(Not) to Read the Bible* is designed to be as personal as it is practical. Each session begins with a brief opening reflection to get you and your group thinking about the topic. You will then watch a video with Dan Kimball, which can be accessed via the streaming code found on the inside front cover. If you are doing the study with a group, you will then engage in some directed discussion. You will close each session with a time of personal reflection and prayer.

If you are doing this study with a group, each person should have his or her own study guide, which includes video teaching notes, group discussion questions, and between-sessions exercises to help you reflect on how you can explore more of the material during the week. You are also encouraged to have a copy of the *How (Not) to Read the Bible* book, as reading it alongside the curriculum will provide you with deeper insights and make the journey more meaningful.

To get the most out of your group experience, keep the following points in mind. First, the real growth in this study will happen during your small-group time. This is where you will process the content of Dan's message, ask questions, and learn from others as you hear what God is doing in their lives.

For this reason, it is important for you to be fully committed to the group and attend each session so you can build trust and rapport with the other members. If you choose to only "go through the motions," or if you refrain from participating, there is a lesser chance you will find what you're looking for during this study.

Second, remember the goal of your small group is to serve as a place where people can share, learn about God, and build intimacy and friendship. For this reason, seek to make your group a "safe place." This means being honest about your thoughts and feelings and listening carefully to everyone else's opinion. Third, resist the temptation to "fix" someone's problem or correct his or her theology, as that's not the purpose of your small-group time. Also, keep everything your group shares confidential. This will foster a rewarding sense of community in your group and create a place where people can heal, be challenged, and grow spiritually.

In between your group times, you can maximize the impact of the course by checking out the personal exploration exercises. This individual time will help you personally reflect and actively respond to the lesson. For each session, you may wish to complete the personal exercises in one sitting or spread it over a few days (for example, working on it a few minutes per day on four different days that week). Note that if you are unable to finish (or even start!) your between-session exercises, you should still attend the group study video session. You are still wanted and welcome at the group even if you don't have your "homework" done.

Keep in mind this study is an opportunity for you to train in a new way of seeing the difficult and confusing parts of the Bible. The videos, discussions, and exercises are simply meant to kickstart your imagination, so you are open to what God wants you to learn about complex passages and how to apply the messages to your life.

Never Read a Bible Verse

(Or You Will Have to Believe in Magical Unicorns)

> *God brought them out of Egypt; he hath as it were the strength of an unicorn.*
>
> **NUMBERS 23:22 KJV**
>
> *And the unicorns shall come down with them . . .*
>
> **ISAIAH 34:7 KJV**

Welcome

When I first tried to read the Bible as a teenager, it seemed more like a work of fiction than anything else—a book filled with epic battles and angels, stories of demons, and even a red dragon.[*] That's why it was placed on a bookshelf between my fantasy and horror books. It fit right in with Bram Stoker's *Dracula* and J. R. R. Tolkien's Lord of the Rings trilogy. As I read and studied

---

[*] 1 Samuel 11:1–11; 2 Samuel 10:10–19; Isaiah 37:36; Revelation 16:12–16; 12:3

more of the Bible in college, I was still disturbed by some of the oddities I found, namely, talking animals. These oddities didn't bode well for someone like me who was trying to make a serious attempt at considering the claims of the Christian faith. The Bible didn't make sense and I was surprised there was so much violence, even in the life of Jesus. I knew that if the Bible was the foundation of Christianity, I had to make sense of these passages.

But making sense of the disturbing passages of the Bible gets complicated in a world full of memes. In addition to seeming anti-women and pro-slavery, it's not hard to find Bible verses that seem to endorse violence, even against babies and small children. And it's not hard to find websites and YouTube videos dedicated to calling out these sorts of Bible verses. What was once known as "The Good Book" is now considered "The Evil Book" by so many. To make matters worse, it's becoming more commonplace to see people quote Bible verses all over the internet and on memed-merchandise to illustrate how strange, crazy, and primitive sounding the Bible is.

If I were reading these bizarre verses for the first time, seeing them in isolation like this, I would feel the same way.

But here's the good news: *there are ways to better understand these crazy-sounding Bible verses.* We must learn how to, and how *not* to, read the Bible. If you are willing to look beyond the visual image and explore beyond a literal, out-of-context reading of a verse, you'll discover the Bible is not "sheer nonsense." The Bible is an amazing, fully inspired, life-changing collection of writings by people who were directed by God through

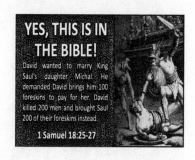

YES, THIS IS IN THE BIBLE!

David wanted to marry King Saul's daughter Michal. He demanded David brings him 100 foreskins to pay for her. David killed 200 men and brought Saul 200 of their foreskins instead.

1 Samuel 18:25-27

God's Spirit. When we read, interpret, and understand the Bible accurately—not just individual verses, but how they fit into the Bible as a whole—our questions and concerns are answered, and we come to better know the author of the Bible. We come to know God.

Watch

Play the video segment for session one (see the streaming video access provided on the inside front cover). As you watch, use the following outline to record any thoughts or concepts that stand out to you.

Video Notes

Questions people are asking about the Bible:

- Is God pro-violence?
- Is the Bible anti-women?
- Is the Bible anti-science?
- Does God endorse slavery?

The Good News: there are reasonable responses to these questions.

Four basic ways to look at the Bible to make sense of these disturbing Bible passages:

1. The Bible is a library, not a book.

   It is a library of books. *It was written by over forty different authors, over 1,500 years, on three continents, in three languages, many different cultural settings, and many different genres.*

   The Holy Spirit is the Author who *guided* the human authors (2 Timothy 3:16; 2 Peter 1:21).

Examining the genres. *The poetry of Song of Solomon 4:15.*

2. The Bible is written for us, not to us.

    Understanding the author's intent and for whom the passage was written. *The dangers of misinterpreting Scripture.*

KEY QUESTIONS TO ASK:

Who was the book or letter of the Bible originally written to?

Why was it written?

What was happening in the world of the original recipients?

What questions were they asking that God was answering to them?

3. Never read a Bible verse in isolation.

Understanding the storyline, the timeline, and the context. *Bible scrolling.*

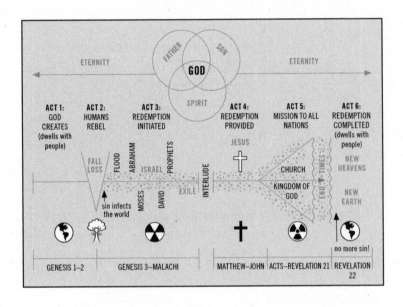

Genesis 1:29 and Genesis 9:3.

4. All the Bible points to Jesus.

The storyline is about Jesus from Genesis to Revelation.

> "This is what I told you while I was still with you: Everything must be fulfilled that is written about me in the Law of Moses, the Prophets and the Psalms."
>
> LUKE 24:44 NIV

What about the unicorns?

Group Discussion

Take a few minutes with your group members to discuss what you just watched and explore these concepts in Scripture.

1. What stood out to you from listening to Dan today? How can you identify with the stories or memes he shared?

2. What questions or concerns do you have about the Bible? Which verses or stories have tripped you up because you don't quite understand the original context?

3. Have you ever considered the Bible as a library of books, rather than a book in the library? How does this shift in mindset change things for you regarding the Bible?

4. Read 2 Timothy 3:14–17. How does Paul encourage Timothy to use the Bible? Why is it worth studying all of the Bible, even with the challenging passages?

5. Placing the challenging verses of Scripture within their proper context is vital to understanding the meaning of these verses. What practices or tools do you use, or could you start using, to make sure you understand the context of a verse or story?

6. Read Isaiah 7:1–17 and Luke 24. What does it mean when Dan says all the Bible points to Jesus? How do we know this to be true?

Reflection

Briefly reflect on the teaching and any notes you took. In the space below, write down your most significant takeaway from this session. Also, consider what discussion question or Bible passage you plan to explore as a result of today's session. If time permits, share it with your group.

Wrap-Up

Pray as a group before you close your time together. Be honest with God about the questions and concerns you have about the sacred text of the Bible. Thank God for creating a library of content written for us even when it's not written to us. Ask God to give you the courage and discipline to explore the context of passages and places in the Bible that seem strange to you. And ask God to give you the vision to see the story of Jesus throughout the entire lens of the Bible.

SESSION ONE

How You Can Respond

Choose at least one of the following suggested activities/reflections to complete over the next week. Consider sharing with your friends or small group members the impact the activity or reflection had on you as you spent this time exploring. Before you begin, you may want to review book chapters 1–3 in *How (Not) to Read the Bible*.

> The primary purpose of reading the Bible is not to know the Bible but to know God.
>
> —JAMES MERRITT

1. Read 2 Peter 1:12–21. When we ignore how a particular verse fits into the context of the entire Bible, we all-too-easily believe that mythical, magical unicorns are in the Bible, too. This makes us susceptible to believing misinformation around things such as talking animals, the way women are viewed in the church, and many other crazy, strange, and weird-sounding things.

The apostle Paul made it clear to his followers that the words of the prophets in the Bible came from God and were carried through the Holy Spirit. While the words of the prophets are true, our interpretations can still go wrong.

Are there any mistruths that this session has made you aware of or things you've believed that you are rethinking? What things have you believed about strange-sounding parts of the Bible that might not actually be true?

2. Visualize the Bible as a library. Imagine walking into a modern-day library and going to the poetry section (*and bonus points if you go to an actual library for this visualization!*). Because of the nature of poetry, you would read it differently than a book in the history section. First, visualize the various sections of the library and imagine how you would approach each section with a different mindset, purpose, and lens. *Do you search in different ways in each section? Do you carry a different kind of purpose or emotion? Do you see things from a different perspective as you visit various corners of the library?*

POETRY

Words with rhythm or rhyme used to communicate in a way that stirs the imagination and emotions.

Colorful words, often exaggerated, to describe ideas or tell stories.

Songs are often written as poetry.

HISTORY

Words and writings documenting events from the past as well as the memory, discovery, collection, organization, presentation, and interpretation of these events as written in books.

REGIONAL

Writings from a particular region of the world during a particular period of time. The region and the time period shape the way writers understood the world and the struggles they faced. The *terms, language, and contexts* differ between regions and time periods.

LAW

Writings detailing laws and cases from different periods of history. Laws may differ and change over time as well as between different geographic regions.

Now visualize the Bible itself as a modern-day library. What section are you drawn to first, and why? What are you searching for? What are you hoping to find? What do you want to learn? How will you know when you've found the story of Jesus in each section?

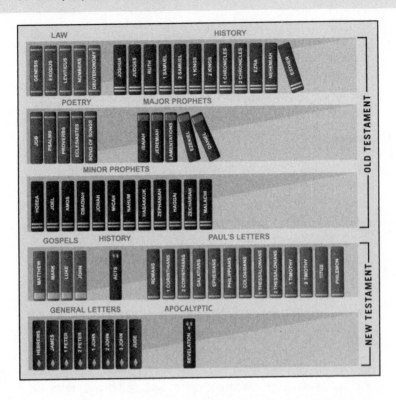

If you're new to exploring the Bible, pick a section that interests you, and start by reading the first book in that section. But don't stop there. Remember, the Bible is meant to be understood within the context of the Bible as a *whole*, not verse by verse.

THE HOLY BIBLE:

Old Testament
New Testament
Sixty-six books
Nine genres
Timespan of 1,500 years.

3. The Bible was written for *all* people at *all* times and it's a sacred source of learning and wisdom. Another way to make sense of this idea is to understand that the Bible was *written for us, but not to us.* While the Bible may not have been written with our contemporary culture and its assumptions and values in mind, that doesn't prevent us from learning and gaining wisdom from the Bible. And the best way to learn the most from the Bible is to read the words and try to hear them as the original audience would have heard them and as the author would have meant them to be understood.

With this in mind, consider which passages or stories stand out to you? Is there a scenario or situation from the Bible you can easily identify with even though you don't live in ancient Israel? Do you see yourself in a Bible character as he or she shares his or her story or cries out to God in prayer? Is there a story that seems like a flashback of your modern-day life? What wisdom have you learned by reading the stories and understanding the characters of the Bible?

POPULAR STORIES FROM THE BIBLE:

Abraham and Sarai (Genesis 16–17)

Jacob and Esau (Genesis 25, 31)

Joseph (Genesis 37)

Moses and Aaron (Exodus 4)

Joshua (Joshua 1)

Deborah (Judges 4–5)

Ruth (book of Ruth)

David (2 Samuel 11, Psalms)

Solomon (2 Kings 1; Song of Songs)

Esther (book of Esther)

Job (book of Job)

Habakkuk (book of Habakkuk)

Mary (Matthew 1; Luke 1)

John the Baptist (Matthew 3; Mark 1; Luke 7; John 1)

Jesus (Mathew, Mark, Luke, John)

The Disciples (Matthew 4, Mark 1, Luke 5, John 1)

The Samaritan Woman (John 4)

Mary and Martha (Luke 10)

Mary Magdalene (Matthew 27; Mark 16; John 20)

The Bleeding Woman (Matthew 9; Mark 5; Luke 8)

Bartimaeus (Mark 10)

Zacchaeus (Luke 10)

Paul (Acts 13)

4. Read Genesis 3:15; 22:18; and Isaiah 53. Most great storylines have a *backstory*—a history or background that builds up to the present moment. Jesus had a backstory, too; one that began long before his birth in Bethlehem. When we see each verse in the Bible as part of a bigger story, we realize just how much we need the Old Testament to understand the New Testament. And what we discover is that *all* of the Bible points to Jesus. There are hints of Jesus in the book of Genesis as far back as the garden of Eden, and later in a promise God made to Abraham. These hints become clearer in the writings of the prophet Isaiah, leading right up to Jesus' birth in the New Testament. This *backstory* gives additional meaning to all that he says and does throughout the Gospel stories of Matthew, Mark, Luke, and John. That's why it's crucial to understand the full story of the Old Testament because it points us to the significance of Jesus and the New Testament he established. Between the *backstory* of the Old Testament and the presence of Jesus, there are six acts to the full story of the Bible.

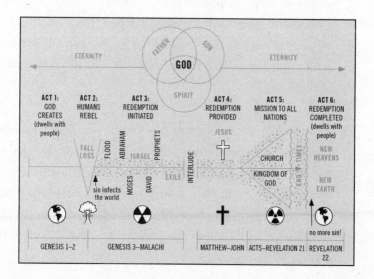

We can't box God into time as we know it, but the events within the Bible as listed here in this historical timeline are as real as our daily experience of life today.

Consider your own story in light of the story of the Bible and Jesus. How many acts are included in your story? How would you label and describe those acts and the events or people who make up those acts? What kind of timeline defines the acts of your story? Which act would you consider your best act so far in life, and your worst? Why is it important for others to understand your story as a whole rather than seeing or experiencing a few small snapshots of your life?

Now that you're beginning to see that it makes a difference knowing where a Bible verse fits into the larger storyline, go back to some of the verses that you find disturbing or difficult to understand. Explore the greater context of those verses and notice how those verses fit into the larger story of the Bible.

5. First, fill out the basic Bible timeline below. Take your best educated guess at placing events and various things listed in the box in the right order on the timeline. You can simply circle the event and draw an arrow, *or* rewrite it on the timeline. Then read "The Storyline of the Bible Comes in Six Acts" on pages 44–54 of the book to see how many events you got in the right order.

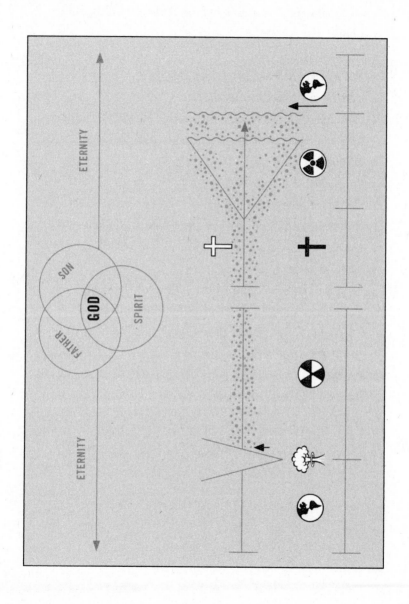

Recommended Resources for Further Study

Dan Kimball, *How (Not) to Read the Bible* (Grand Rapids: Zondervan, 2020).

Practical resources about finding Jesus throughout the entire Bible, not just the four Gospels:

Dan Kimball, *Adventures in Churchland: Finding Jesus in the Mess of Organized Religion* (Grand Rapids: Zondervan, 2012).

If you're interested in examining the story structure of the Bible, check out:

The Bible Project, "The Story of the Bible" study notes on the six-act play structure in *How to Read the Bible*, www .thebibleproject.org.

Craig G. Bartholomew and Michael W. Goheen, *The Drama of Scripture: Finding Our Place in the Biblical Story.*

N. T. Wright, *Scripture and the Authority of God.*

For Next Week: Before your group's next session, read chapters 4–6 in *How (Not) to Read the Bible.*

Stranger Things

Shrimp, Slavery, and Skin of a Dead Pig

> *Do your best to present yourself to God as one approved, a worker who does not need to be ashamed and who correctly handles the word of truth.*
>
> 2 TIMOTHY 2:15 NIV

Welcome

For many people today, reading Bible verses with strange, even horrifying sounding laws and commands, can be confusing and upsetting. Some verses make no sense to us or even seem contrary to what we imagine God to be like. There are verses that seem to approve of things like slavery, polygamy, killing birds to cure mold, bloody rituals, and extreme violence towards people and animals. *Weird and confusing, right?* But when we dive in and look beneath the surface, even the most strange or off-putting verses begin to make sense. This is why we talked in the last session about never reading a bible verse without reading the verses around it to understand the context, especially in the Old Testament.

Since so many of the "strange" verses are from the early Old Testament books of the Bible, such as Exodus, Leviticus, and Deuteronomy, we need to look at what was happening more specifically in those books. To apply the principles from the last session, we need to *never read a Bible verse* and *remember that the Bible was written for us, but not to us*. Starting with these principles allows us to see details in the text that make a major difference in our search to make sense of these verses. When we see the real context of these complicated passages, we see how each book of the Bible was written to a specific group of people in a specific place. It's in that specific place with a specific group of people where these strange laws start to make sense in the greater story of the Bible as a whole.

These "stranger things" of the Old Testament would have made perfect sense to the ancient Israelites. They would have understood how God was instructing them to remain distinct from the practices of other people groups in the region—to remain holy as they entered the promised land. God gave the Israelites strange laws and practices to remind them each day how they were different from other people groups who worshiped other gods.

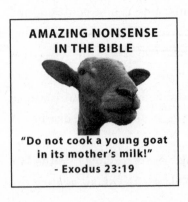

AMAZING NONSENSE IN THE BIBLE

"Do not cook a young goat in its mother's milk!"
- Exodus 23:19

When we do the hard work of understanding the full context of the laws of the Old Testament and what Jesus had to say about these old laws in the New Testament, we see that many of these verses do not apply to the followers of Jesus today. So, when loud critics and critical memes attempt to convince us that the Bible is irrelevant for us today, what they are actually communicating is a misunderstanding and extreme misuse of the Bible. That's why we are going to closely examine the "stranger things" of the Old Testament today, particularly questions and criticisms about shrimp, slavery, and the skin of a dead pig.

Watch

Play the video segment for session two (see the streaming video access provided on the inside front cover). As you watch, use the following outline to record any thoughts or concepts that stand out to you.

Video Notes:

Cherry-picking Bible verses.

Things "banned" in the Bible.

KEY QUESTIONS TO ASK: Why does God include these bizarre-sounding restrictions?

Making Sense of These Strange Verses:
The Bible is a library, not a book.

QUESTION: Which section and shelf are these strange verses from?
ANSWER: The Law Books

The Bible was written for us, not to us.

QUESTION: Why were these laws written—to whom, when, and why?
ANSWER: These laws were written to the Israelites, between 1550–1069 B.C.

> "You shall be holy, for I the LORD your God am holy."
> LEVITICUS 19:2 ESV

HISTORIC LAWS IN THE US

Arizona: It is illegal for a donkey to sleep in a bathtub
Kentucky: It is illegal to carry ice cream in your back pocket
Rhode Island: It is illegal to throw pickle juice on a trolley
Maryland: It is illegal to mistreat oysters

What makes sense about Leviticus: God was giving instruction to a specific group of people at a specific time.

The Backstory:

"Do not bow down before their gods or worship them or follow their practices."

Exodus 23:24 NIV

"Do not let them live in your land or they will cause you to sin against me, because the worship of their gods will certainly be a snare to you."

Exodus 23:33 NIV

"Be careful not to make a treaty with those who live in the land; for when they prostitute themselves to their gods and sacrifice to them, they will invite you and you will eat their sacrifices. And when you choose some of their daughters as wives for your sons and those daughters prostitute themselves to their gods, they will lead your sons to do the same."

Exodus 34:15–16 NIV

Keeping Things Separate, On Purpose:

"Keep my decrees. Do not mate different kinds of animals. Do not plant your field with two kinds of seed. Do not wear clothing woven of two kinds of material."

Leviticus 19:19 NIV

"Do not plant two kinds of seed in your vineyard; if you do, not only the crops you plant but also the fruit of the vineyard will be defiled. Do not plow with ox and a donkey yoked together. Do not wear clothes of wool and linen woven together."

Deuteronomy 22:9–11 NIV

Back to the shrimp: *Dietary laws keep the Israelites separate from others.*

> God wants his people to remain loyal to him, the one true God.

KEY QUESTION: Do these rules stop at the Old Testament, or are we supposed to be practicing them today?
ANSWER: Some rules stop and some don't.

Before Jesus' time, God's people, as recounted in the Old Testament, had to offer sacrifices to atone for sin and follow a complex set of rules for ceremonial purity and cleanliness. This included eating certain kinds of foods while abstaining from others, like shellfish, and wearing certain forms of dress garments woven with two kinds of material. That was the only way one could approach God in worship. Today, such rules are not followed by Christians because of what Jesus Christ did on the Cross. In short, the coming of Christ changed how we worship, but not how we live. The moral law outlines God's own character: his integrity, love, and faithfulness. And so everything the Old Testament says about loving our neighbor, caring for the poor, generosity with our possessions, social relationships, and commitment to our family is still enforced.

If the New Testament has reaffirmed a commandment, then it is still in force for us today.

Tim Keller, Pastor and Author

KEY QUESTION: What about slavery?
ANSWER: According to the Old Testament and New Testament, slavery is *wrong*.

"Anyone who kidnaps someone is to be put to death, whether the victim has been sold or is still in the kidnapper's possession."

Exodus 21:16 NIV

"We also know that the law is made not for the righteous but for lawbreakers and rebels, the ungodly and sinful, the unholy and irreligious, for those who kill their fathers or mothers, for murderers, for the sexually immoral, for those practicing homosexuality, for slave traders and liars and perjurers—and for whatever else is contrary to the sound doctrine."

1 Timothy 1:9–10 NIV

Understanding the use of the term *slavery:* slaves in the Old Testament were more like servants, or bondservants.

A *servant* or *bondservant* is someone who sold themselves to pay a debt or escape poverty.

DID YOU KNOW?

Slavery in the New Testament: Thirty percent of the population were servants.

The story of Philemon and Onesimus, as told by Paul:

"No longer as a slave, but better than a slave, as a dear brother. He is very dear to me but even dearer to you, both as a fellow man and as a brother in the Lord."

Philemon 1:16 NIV

Although Christians could not abolish Roman slavery, they started a new form of society within the Roman empire, and effectively challenged the status of human beings either as masters or slaves to other human beings. Christians were the ones that lead the abolishment of slavery.

REMEMBER THIS: The New Testament laid the groundwork to abolish slavery and taught that all humans have equal worth.

Group Discussion:

Take a few minutes with your group members to discuss what you just watched and explore these concepts in Scripture.

1. What stood out to you from listening to Dan today? How can you identify with the questions or criticisms he shared?

2. What other questions does this teaching session bring up for you? Are there confusing parts of Scripture not mentioned by Dan that you'd like to better understand?

3. How would you respond if a friend brought up hard-to-understand Bible topics such as *shrimp, slavery,* and the *skin of a dead pig*? What other Bible criticisms do you hear?

4. Read 1 Timothy 1:1–11. What are the "controversial speculations" and "meaningless talk" Paul refers to in this passage? For whom was the law made, and what kind of encouragement does Paul give Timothy? How is this encouragement true for us today?

5. Read Philemon 1. Paul writes a plea to Philemon on behalf of Onesimus. What do you notice about Paul's posture towards Philemon, and Paul's relationship with Onesimus? In what ways does it help to understand the context around Paul's use of the term "slave"?

6. Dan mentions how critics believe the Bible condones slavery, and yet "no longer a slave" appears in several key Bible passages: Leviticus 26:13, Jeremiah 34:10, Romans 6:6, and Galatians 4:7. As you read these verses and skim around them for context, what insights do you notice? Why does this phrase matter?

Reflection

Briefly reflect on the teaching and any notes you took. In the space below, write down your most significant takeaway from this session. Also, consider what discussion question or Bible passage you're going to explore as a result of today's session. If time permits, share it with your group.

Wrap-Up

Pray as a group before you close your time together. Be honest with God about the questions and concerns you may still have about the Bible. Thank God for the backstory of the Bible—that we can read and research to understand what has been written for us even when it's not written to us. Ask God to give you the desire to lean into the confusing laws and complex language of Scripture. And ask God to give you clarity in understanding which Old Testament laws still stand true, and which ones have been abolished for New Testament laws established by Jesus.

How You Can Respond

Choose at least one of the following suggested activities/reflections to complete over the next week. Consider sharing with your friends or small group members the impact the activity or reflection had on you as you spent this time exploring. Before you begin, you may want to review book chapters 4–6 in *How (Not) to Read the Bible.*

> When Jesus came, everything changed, and from the time of Jesus onward, we have to look at everything in the Bible through a new lens of interpretation.

1. It's common to read the "stranger things" of Old Testament laws and wonder if we even want to be Christians! A question pastors hear often after their churchgoers read Leviticus 19:28 is this: *Is it okay to be a Christian and get a tattoo?* Read the backstory in "If These Laws Were Only for Israel at the Time, Do They Apply to Us Today?" on pages 78–79 of *How (Not) To Read The Bible.*

According to Dan, why are tattoos outlawed for the Israelites in Leviticus? And what does this mean for us today?

The Old Testament isn't the only place where we read "stranger things" in Scripture—they appear in the New Testament, too. Read 1 Corinthians 11:1–16. What strange rules appear here? How do Christians respond to this rule today?

2. Is the Bible credible and trustworthy? This is the underlying question behind the criticisms we've been talking about in Session Two.

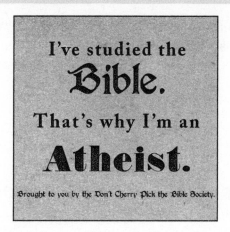

I've studied the
Bible.
That's why I'm an
Atheist.
Brought to you by the Don't Cherry Pick the Bible Society.

When we look at the context of the greater story of the Gospel in light of the strange verses we read, we see that God is credible and trustworthy. In the first five books of the Bible, God instructed Moses to write down the history of the Israelites to teach them it was God who created everything, not the gods of neighboring Egyptians or other gods. God wanted the Israelites to pattern their lives after him, not other nations who worshipped and followed other gods. So God establishes his credibility and trustworthiness by reminding the Israelites who he is as the creator of the universe (Exodus 3:15–17, Isaiah 45:12) and who they are as image bearers of God (Genesis 1:27).

What makes the Bible credible and trustworthy from your perspective?

What principles can you remember when you encounter strange things in the Bible?

3. Read Leviticus 20. According to this passage, in what ways were the Israelites "set apart" from neighboring nations and why?

THE WAYS	THE WHY

4. Read "Why Do We Follow Some Commands but Not Others"
    on pages 81–85 in the book *How (Not) To Read The Bible*. In
    the following graphic, you can see where the Old Testament
    law arrow ends on the timeline. It stops with the death and
    resurrection of Jesus, which means all of the strange, bizarre
    stuff stops, too. No more strict dietary laws, weird worship
    rituals, sacrifices, etc. And then, a new arrow starts with
    Jesus. This is the start of the new law, otherwise known as
    the law of Jesus.

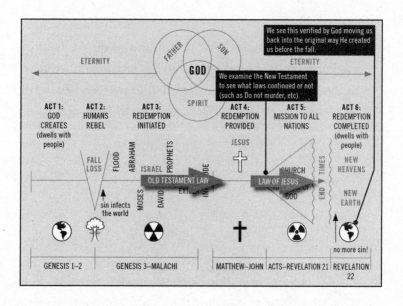

Read Galatians 3:23–28; 6:2; and 1 Corinthians 9:21.
What insights stand out about the new law of Jesus?

Read Matthew 28:16–20 and Matthew 22:36–40. According to these two passages, how would you summarize the new "law" of Jesus?

Read 1 Corinthians 13. What similarities do you hear or see between the law of Jesus and the love described here by the Apostle Paul? Where do you find yourself lacking in love based on these descriptions of love by Jesus and Paul?

5. The Israelites weren't the only ones with "stranger things" in their laws. Strange sounding things pop up in our modern context, too—whether it's actual laws or the societal rules we strive to live by. *What laws or rules are the "stranger things" of our modern day (even things that make perfect sense to us today but might be specific to who we are as a generation, living in this specific time)? If you're having a hard time answering these questions, then do a quick online search for "US laws that make no sense."*

MODERN DAY "STRANGER THINGS" LAWS & RULES	THE MEANING OR PURPOSE OF THESE RULES

Recommended Resources for Further Study

Practical resources for finding a loving God
in Old Testament history and law:

Genesis, a Zondervan Illustrated Bible Backgrounds Commentary
by John H. Walton, ed. (Grand Rapids: Zondervan, 2009),
pg. 246.

*Is God a Moral Monster? Making Sense of the Old Testament
God* by Paul Copan (Grand Rapids: Baker, 2011).

"Old Testament Law and the Charge of Inconsistency" article
by Tim Keller *https://timothykeller.com/blog/2012/6/12
/old-testament-law-and-the-charge-of-inconsistency.*

If you're interested in seeing how modern culture feeds
into the "stranger things" criticisms, check out:

The West Wing, season 2, episode 3, "The Midterms."

"Things the Bible Bans" google search for popular YouTube
    videos, blogs and articles about misunderstandings and
    misuse of the complex passages of the Bible.

For Next Week: Before your group's next session, read chapters 7–9
in *How (Not) to Read the Bible*.

Boys' Club Christianity

Is the Bible Anti-Women?

> *There is neither Jew nor Gentile, neither slave nor free, nor is there male and female, for you are all one in Christ Jesus.*
>
> GALATIANS 3:28 NIV

Welcome

We live in a world today where there is a recognition and intolerance of misogyny in our society. As Christians, we should add our support out of love and justice to affirm women's rights to equal respect, value, and worth. But it starts to get uncomfortable when critics talk about Bible verses that—at face value—seem to demean and devalue women.

Misogyny refers to contempt for and prejudice against women.

Sadly, there have been—and still are—some churches and Christians who misuse the text to perpetuate misogyny and patriarchy. But when you study the Scriptures and seek to understand them in their cultural context, it's clear that the Bible is actually an *advocate* for women rather than a weapon against women. From the beginning, we see that God created men and women to represent him and make a difference in the world. We see how God created us uniquely as men and women, as equals, to serve God with whatever gifts he's given us.

Note: We do see differences in the contemporary church's beliefs about whether men and women both can serve in what are called "offices" of the church such as "pastor" and "elder". Different churches have different leadership structures that are too complex to discuss for the purpose of this study. There are healthy churches who highly respect and honor women who hold differing views on this. For this study, we won't be going into church leadership so please talk to the leaders of your church to see what specific beliefs they have. For this study, we will be focusing on looking at the disturbing and confusing sounding verses that seem to directly be anti-women.

As we've established in the first two sessions, *never read a Bible verse*. Which means, we need to understand the backstory of these strange and confusing verses about women before we can interpret them. Seeing these verses within their original context reveals that God didn't create or endorse misogyny, patriarchy, or female oppression. Those evils resulted from the human rebellion that happened at the fall in the garden of Eden. Humans chose to go against God's original design, one in which men and women were created equal. And as a result, men used their power to establish an unequal hierarchy over women. Ever since then, God has been making changes to restore things back to the way they were in the beginning of time.

Today we'll look at how God worked within the cultural institutions and social patterns of ancient Israel—not approving of them, but rather transforming them. We'll see how God directly confronted an ancient era where humans lived in a female-oppressed world. And we will see how massive changes took place when Jesus showed up on the scene. The New Testament made it even more clear that God did not see women as subordinate or of lesser value than men. Rather, it portrays a future that returns us to the original harmony of the garden where men and women live as co-equals and as image-bearers of God.

Watch

Play the video segment for session three (see the streaming video access provided on the inside front cover). As you watch, use the following outline to record any thoughts or concepts that stand out to you.

Video Notes:

KEY QUESTION: Is the Bible Anti-Women?

A woman should learn in quietness and full submission. I do not permit a woman to teach or to assume authority over a man; she must be quiet.

1 Timothy 2:11–12 NIV

Women should remain silent in the churches. They are not allowed to speak, but must be in submission, as the law says. If they want to inquire about something, they should ask their own husbands at home; for it is disgraceful for a woman to speak in the church.

1 Corinthians 14:34–35 NIV

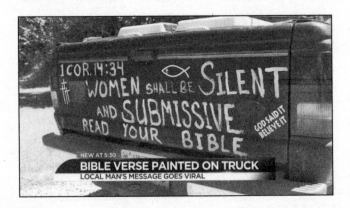

KEY QUESTION: Is it true women are supposed to just be the helpers?

The Lord God said, "It is not good for the man to be alone. I will make a helper suitable for him."

Genesis 2:18 NIV

Heroes of Faith and a common view of women.

> *Concubine* means a woman who lives with
> a man (in polygamous societies) but has
> lower status than his wife or wives.

Back to the Beginning: The timeline of the Bible.

So God created mankind in his own image, in the image of
God he created them; male and female he created them. God
blessed them and said to them, "Be fruitful and increase in
number; fill the earth and subdue it. Rule over the fish in the
sea and the birds in the sky and over every living creature that
moves on the ground."

Genesis 1:27–28 NIV

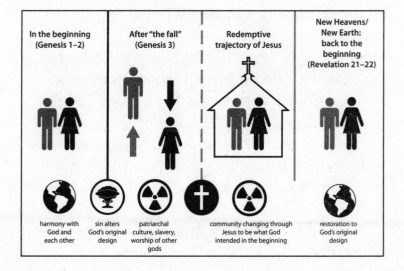

> *Ezer* means "helper" in Hebrew. It appears twenty times in the Old Testament, and nearly every time it refers to God.

We wait in hope for the Lord; he is our help and our shield.
Psalm 33:20 NIV

> *Helper* means savior, rescuer, protector. It's used to define God's relationship with humans.

> *Ezer* does not mean women are subservient to men, rather they are co-equal and serve God together.

KEY QUESTION: Are women responsible for the Fall?

> The Fall refers to the loss, or falling away of the beautiful harmonious relationship humans had with God and the loss of being in his intimate presence.

Human rebellion: *Sin and ego entered the world as a result of the Fall.*

One of the consequences of the Fall: *Men began overpowering women.*

A patriarchal culture developed. But this is not what God created in the beginning.

We see stories in the Old Testament of when God was raising up women and peeking through the patriarchy in the Old Testament.

WOMEN OF THE OLD TESTAMENT:

Miriam: a prophet and the sister of Moses (Exodus 15, Micah 6:4)

Deborah: a judge and military leader (Judges 4)

Huldah: a respected, sought-after prophet (2 Kings 22)

Rahab: a prostitute who responded to God (Joshua 2 and 6, Hebrews 11:31)

Jesus starts making change:

> After this, Jesus traveled about from one town and village to another, proclaiming the good news of the kingdom of God. The Twelve were with him, and also some women who had been cured of evil spirits and diseases: Mary (called Magdalene) from whom seven demons had come out; Joanna the wife of Chuza, the manager of Herod's household; Susanna; and many others. These women were helping to support them out of their own means.
>
> *Luke 8:1–3 NIV (1984)*

Paul and the Church follow the way Jesus treats women:

WOMEN OF THE NEW TESTAMENT:

Junia: outstanding among the apostles (Romans 16:6–7)

Lydia: hosted and led the early church (Acts 16)

Four daughters of Philip: prophetesses (Acts 21)

Priscilla: a teacher and leader of the early church (Acts 18:26)

Phoebe: a deacon in the early church, entrusted with a letter to the Romans (Romans 16:1–2)

Clearly, the trajectory of the whole Bible shows how women and men are both gifted and called co-equals to be serving Jesus in this world and are of great worth.

Back to the verses in the beginning of this session:

To understand the backstory of strange verses in the Bible, look at:

Who was it written to?
Why?
What genre?

Women praying and prophesying (1 Corinthians 12 and 13)

Women were learning to pray in a calm, receptive manner, rather than be silent (1 Timothy 2)

Silence means *"tranquility"* in Hebrew

Like the saying, "don't swim after eating," it seems like women are being asked not to teach until they learn and are properly trained.

Authority means "usurp or violently overthrow" in Greek

It seems as though Paul is helping women in the church lead in a way different from the authoritarian feminism surge of the day.

Throughout the Bible, God is restoring his original design for men and women to co-equally serve God together in this world.

Group Discussion

Take a few minutes with your group members to discuss what you just watched and explore these concepts in Scripture.

1. What stood out to you from listening to Dan today? What questions or answers about the Bible's teaching about women were made clear to you in this session?

2. How have these strange verses regarding women been misconstrued by society and by the church?

3. How have you misunderstood any of the Bible's view of women? How has this misunderstanding impacted you personally? Your family? Your church?

4. Read Psalm 33:20 and Genesis 2:18. How does the use of *ezer*—the Hebrew word for helper—for both God and the first woman inspire you? How does it change your understanding of the role of women?

5. Read Judges 4. This story isn't just about Deborah, it's about another woman, too. Who else is in this story, and why is this story so culturally significant for these two women?

6. Read Romans 16. The apostle Paul, often criticized for his New Testament views, sends a letter to the Romans encouraging them to properly greet early church workers, many of them *women*. How are women significantly contributing to the church today?

Reflection

Briefly reflect on the teaching and any notes you took. In the space below, write down your most significant takeaway from this session. Also, consider what discussion question or Bible passage you're going to explore as a result of today's session. If time permits, share it with your group.

Wrap-Up

Pray as a group before you close your time together. Be honest with God about the ways you've been impacted by or contributed to a wrong view of women according to a misinformed interpretation of Scripture. Thank God for creating both men and women in God's likeness—even referring to women as "ezers" a term God uses to describe himself, too. Ask God to give you clarity and wisdom when you encounter misconstrued views where women are not treated as equals. May God give you courage to speak up for the women around you. And for the men, ask God to show you ways you can treat women with equality and serve on mission together.

How You Can Respond

Choose at least one of the following suggested activities/reflections to complete over the next week. Consider sharing with your friends or small group members the impact the activity or reflection had on you as you spent this time exploring. Before you begin, you may want to review book chapters 7–9 in *How (Not) to Read the Bible*.

> When you look into the backstory to understand the cultural background, there is sense to be made from what sounds so strange to us. You can have confidence that these Bible verses also have legitimate interpretations.

1. Read Genesis 3. After the fall of human rebellion (also known as "original sin") God describes to Adam and Eve what they would experience from then on: *painful toil, painful childbirth, and a struggle to subdue the earth.* We also see the first evidence of human selfishness and blame-shifting (vs. 12–13). It is here that a selfish hierarchy replaces the harmony of the original creation.

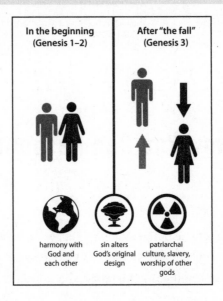

In the beginning (Genesis 1–2)	After "the fall" (Genesis 3)
harmony with God and each other	sin alters God's original design · patriarchal culture, slavery, worship of other gods

Have you ever considered Genesis 3 as the start of patriarchy in society as we know it today, and how does this perspective change things for you? Why is it significant to understand that this hierarchy occurs after the fall of Adam and Eve?

Have you had any personal experiences or observations of when you have either stood against misogyny or even seen it perpetuated? In what ways has this been encouraging or discouraging to you and/or the women around you?

2. Read Romans 5:12 and 1 Timothy 2. Paul, the author of both passages, clearly believed both Adam and Eve were equally to blame for the fall.

Why do you think Eve gets most of the blame in our cultural interpretation of Genesis 3?

How do these verses illuminate your understanding of this common misunderstanding?

What can you do to see the furthering of the equality of the value and worth of women using the context of the larger story of the Bible as your foundation?

3. Read "Glimpses of Equality and Hope in a Patriarchal Fallout Culture" on pages 116–119 in the book *How (Not) to Read the Bible*. Paul's perspective in the previous exercise is evidence that, even as we acknowledge the sad and horrific results of the fall and how it impacted the relationship of men and women, we also see that God did not abandon women by endorsing cultural patriarchy. Patriarchy was never God's intention, as with slavery, and over time he was working to change hearts and overturn the evil effects of human sin. In doing so, God raised up women to be prophets, teachers, leaders, and examples to all humankind in an era ruled mostly by men.

What stands out to you as you skim the stories of these women in the Old Testament? In what ways do these stories highlight God's view of women in ancient Israel? And how did these women contribute to significant change in the world at the time?

Miriam (Exodus 15, Micah 6:4)

Deborah (Judges 4–5)

Huldah (2 Kings 22)

The Working Woman of ancient Israel (Proverbs 31)

Joel's Prophecy (Joel 2:28–29)

Esther (Book of Esther, namely chapters 2 and 8)

Ruth (Book of Ruth)

4. Read "Jesus, the Rabbi who Hangs Out with Women" on pages 122–124. Jesus also lived in a culture where women were not generally treated with the same respect, worth, and value as men. And these views weren't just limited to Jewish culture—they were just as common in Greek and Roman culture, too. But we see Jesus and his followers continuing the trajectory of restoring God's original creation intentions, including the equality of women with men. When we read how Jesus interacted with women, we need to understand how countercultural, highly shocking, and extremely challenging this was for the religious leaders of the day. Much to

their surprise and concern, Jesus treated women with respect, dignity, and equality.

Read John 4:1–42, and John 8:1–11. What's so surprising about the way Jesus interacts with the Samaritan woman?

Read John 12:1–11. What stands out about the way Jesus interacts with Judas and Mary? How do you think both of them felt after their encounter with Jesus?

Read Luke 8:1–3. In what ways were the disciples indebted to the women who followed Jesus with them? How do you imagine this dynamic shifted the cultural perspective of these men and the women who supported them?

Read Luke 24:1–11. Why would Jesus work against Jewish law by revealing his resurrected self to women who were not allowed to bear legal witness? Why was this significant in the immediate moment for the disciples? And how is this significant for the church today?

5. Read "The Church Extends What Jesus Started, through Both Men and Women" on pages 125–127 in the book, and then read Acts 2. After Jesus, as the church was being born, we see the Holy Spirit working through the followers of Jesus. No longer was the Spirit limited to the temple in Jerusalem or just a few people, but the Spirit now dwelled in those who put their faith in Jesus. In fact, the very first event in the new church is a sermon by Peter in which he reminds his Jewish listeners of the prophecy of Joel (vs. 17–18).

What stands out to you about the stories of Phoebe, Priscilla and her husband, Aquila, and the list of women Paul mentioned in Romans 16?

How do the spiritual gifts given by God through the Holy Spirit to all believers "level the playing field" between men and women?

For just as each of us has one body with many members, and these members do not all have the same function, so in Christ we, though many, form one body, and each member belongs to all the others. We have different gifts, according to the grace given to each of us.

If your gift is prophesying, then prophesy in accordance with your faith;

if it is serving, then serve;

if it is teaching, then teach;

if it is to encourage, then give encouragement;

if it is giving, then give generously;

if it is to lead, do it diligently;

if it is to show mercy, do it cheerfully.

ROMANS 12:4–8 NIV

In what ways has the modern church limited the practice of these spiritual gifts by requiring women to fulfill some, and men to fulfill others, without equality of practice in all of the gifts?

Based on this list (and regardless of your gender), which spiritual gifts has God given you to serve his kingdom and the world? How are you practicing those gifts?

Recommended Resources for Further Study

Practical resources for making sense of the
anti-women verses in the Bible:

The Blue Parakeet: Rethinking How You Read the Bible, 2nd
    Edition by Scot McKnight (Grand Rapids: Zondervan, 2018).
Paul Behaving Badly: Was the Apostle Paul a Racist, Chauvinist
    Jerk? By E. Randolph Richards and Brandon J. O'Brien
    (Downers Grove, IL: InterVarsity, 2016).

If you're interested in understanding the worldview
according to ancient Jewish customs:

Every Man's Talmud by Abraham Cohen (New York: Schocken,
    1949).
IVP Bible Background Commentary: New Testament by Craig
    S. Keener (Downers Grove, IL: InterVarsity, 1993).

For Next Week: Before your group's next session, read chapters 10–12 in *How (Not) to Read the Bible.*

Jesus Riding a Dinosaur

Is the Bible Anti-Science?

> *In the beginning God created the heavens and the earth.*
>
> GENESIS 1:1 NIV

Welcome

The Bible has often been mocked, especially when it comes to a scientific perspective, but that's only because we need to learn how (not) to read the Bible. So often the most common critiques of the crazy-sounding Bible passages from the creation story are not all that crazy when you look a little deeper to learn what God is actually saying. When we pull verses out of context and fail to put in the time and effort to understand what the author is trying to say, we can come up with some great anti-science memes.

CHRISTIANITY:
The belief that some cosmic Jewish Zombie can make you live forever if you symbolically eat his flesh and telepathically tell him that you accept him as your master, so he can remove an evil source from your soul that is present in humanity because a rib-woman was convinced by a talking snake to eat from a magical tree.

Makes perfect sense.

63

But these memes do not accurately represent what the Bible is saying in those verses.

Despite how often it happens, the first few chapters of Genesis were not written to explain the scientific process of how God created everything. They were written to simply communicate to the ancient Israelites that everything they could see in the air and on land and everything they knew was made by God. When we read Genesis through the eyes of the Israelites and understand the purpose for which this book was written, we can allow for many interpretations and options in the story of creation.

Something to always remember is that God does defy science throughout the Bible. The resurrection of Jesus goes against what we know of science. Jesus walking on water and the many miracles we see in the Bible does go against science. But so much of the arguing and mocking about science and the Bible usually is about the early chapters of Genesis. One of my goals in this session is to help you see that there is no need to have to choose between Christianity and science with the creation story. Because there are various viewpoints of the creation story doesn't mean some of us lack full trust in the Bible, nor does it mean we doubt God or refuse to take his Word seriously. Just the opposite. Studying why a book was written and to whom, and learning

about the context and cultural world in which it was written is what allows us to place our full trust in God. It is taking the Scriptures seriously by making sure we understand what God is saying. It is a commitment to truth, not a lessening of the truth.

God communicates his truth to the ancient Israelites with poetry and symbolism, not through a scientific medical lens. When we're willing to put ourselves in the shoes of the ancient Israelites, then we can understand the awesome power and beautiful purpose for everything through the poetic movement and symmetry of the creation story. So the next time you see a meme for Jesus riding a dinosaur, a talking snake, or a literal description of the creation story, remember—*there is more happening there.* Let's take a closer look.

Watch

Play the video segment for session four (see the streaming video access provided on the inside front cover). As you watch, use the following outline to record any thoughts or concepts that stand out to you.

Video Notes:
Jesus Riding a Dinosaur

KEY QUESTION: Can we trust the validity of the Bible when compared to Science?

Myth: We must choose between the Bible and Science.

The Bible is filled with incredible miracles and amazing things that defy what we know of science.

Confusing Bible Verses

> Then the LORD God made a woman from the rib he had taken
> out of the man, and he brought her to the man.
>
> *Genesis 2:22 NIV*

The Sequence and Order of Creation: Genesis 1

The question is not God's ability, but whether or not we understand what he is telling us.

The importance of knowing *how to* and *how not to* read the Bible:

Remembering the Context:

Why are these chapters in the Bible?
What is their purpose in the larger story?

I realized that all my life, I had been reading Genesis from the perspective of the modern person. I had read it through the lens of a historically sophisticated, scientifically influenced individual. I assumed Genesis was written to answer the questions of origins that people are asking today.

But I had never asked the most important vital question of all: What did Moses mean when we wrote this text? After all, "my Bible" was Moses' "Bible" first. Was Moses acquainted with Charles Darwin? . . . Was he writing to discredit any modern theory of evolution? Were his readers troubled by calculations of the speed of light and the distance of the galaxies from earth? Were they puzzling over the significance of DNA? Were they debating a young earth versus an old earth? Would they have had any inkling about a modern scientific worldview?

If you agree that the answer to these questions is obviously no, then the logical question is, what was on their minds? How would they have understood Genesis 1? . . . *What did Genesis mean to the original author and original readers?*

—EXCERPT FROM *IN THE BEGINNING . . . WE MISUNDERSTOOD*

BY JOHNNY MILLER AND JOHN SODEN

KEY QUESTION: Who was Genesis written to?

ANSWER: the people of Israel after slavery in Egypt for 400 years

---

OUR QUESTIONS TODAY:

How old is the Earth?

Did Creation really take place in six 24-hour time periods?

What about the fossil record, transitional forms and evolution?

Could primitive nucleic and amino acids have laid the foundation for cellular biochemistry?

Were there dinosaurs on the Ark?

Did Adam have a belly button?

THE LIKELY QUESTIONS OF THE ISRAELITES:

Are we going to survive in the desert?

Is there really one God? What about the Egyptian gods?

What do we have to do to please this one God?

Should we worship our God like the Egyptians and Canaanites worship their gods?

We must pay attention to the *literary-artistic design* of the Hebrew text.

> Now the earth was formless and empty, darkness was over the surface of the deep, and the Spirit of God was hovering over the waters.
>
> *Genesis 1:2 NIV*

God's Work	Problem: Creation is "formless and empty" (1:2).	
	Forming	**Filling**
	Day 1: light and darkness	Day 4: the lights of day and night
	Day 2: sky and sea	Day 5: birds and fish
	Day 3: fertile earth	Day 6: land animals, including man
	Result: The work of creation is finished, and God can rest (2:1).	

God brought order to chaos through the symmetry of Creation.

The 24-hour Debate.

DAY = *YOM* IN HEBREW

Twelve hours and half a day in Genesis 1:5

a whole week in Genesis 2:2

a growing season, probably several months in Genesis 4:3

an eternity in Genesis 44:32

a physical lifetime in Genesis 43:9 and Deut. 4:40 and 19:9

a time period equal to forty days in Deuteronomy 10:10

Thought of the ancient days: *the Earth as stationary, and the Sun as revolving*

> The sun rises and the sun sets,
>> and hurries back to where it rises.
>
> *Ecclesiastes 1:5 NIV*

The LORD reigns, he is robed in majesty;
> the LORD is robed in majesty and armed with strength;
> Indeed, the world is established, firm and secure.
>> *Psalm 93:1 NIV*

Tremble before him, all the earth!
> The world is firmly established; it cannot be moved.
>> *1 Chronicles 16:30 NIV*

GALILEO, THE FATHER OF MODERN SCIENCE (1632): *THE EARTH ORBITS AROUND THE SUN*

June 22, 1633:

We pronounce, judge, and declare that you, the said Galileo, have rendered yourself vehemently suspected by this Holy Office of heresy, that is, of having believed and held the doctrine (which is false and contrary to the Holy and Divine Scriptures) that the sun is the center of the world, and that it does not move from east to west, and that the earth does move and is not the center of the world.

Genesis uses common, everyday language to communicate truth to the world; it does not make a scientific statement.

We need to be careful not to import scientific meaning or draw scientific conclusions from the Bible when it isn't meant to be read that way.

> The Bible teaches us how to go to heaven, not how the heavens go.
> —GALILEO

Group Discussion:

Take a few minutes with your group members to discuss what you just watched and explore these concepts in Scripture.

1. What stood out to you from listening to Dan today? What questions or answers about science and creation were made clear to you in this session?

2. According to Dan, how can we trust the validity of the Bible when compared to Science?

3. What perspectives change for you when you see the book of Genesis explained through the lens of the literary-artistic design of the Hebrew text? Why is it important to understand that Genesis was written to Israelites after they had been in slavery?

4. Read Genesis 1. How might the Creation story of Genesis be told if it were written today through the lens of modern science and our understanding of evolution?

5. Read Ecclesiastes 3:1–11. Here is another place in Scripture where we see the literary-artistic design of the text that considers our human experience "from beginning to end." How does this passage mimic Genesis 1? How does it differ?

6. Read 1 Corinthians 2:6–16. According to the Apostle Paul, how do we understand and interpret everything God has given us in this world, including Earth as God's creation? How can we trust the truth of the Bible if it's not a scientific statement?

Reflection

Briefly reflect on the teaching and any notes you took. In the space below, write down your most significant takeaway from this session. Also, consider what discussion question or Bible passage you're going to explore as a result of today's session. If time permits, share it with your group.

Wrap-Up

Pray as a group before you close your time together. Be honest with God about the questions and concerns you may still have about Creation and the Bible. Thank God for the truth of the Bible, and for the wisdom to see this truth beyond the scientific statements we may still seek. Ask God to give you clarity in understanding the spiritual truths of the Bible, even when those truths are beyond your human experience of scientific truth.

SESSION FOUR

How You Can Respond

Choose at least one of the following suggested activities/reflections to complete over the next week. Consider sharing with your friends or small group members the impact the activity or reflection had on you as you spent this time exploring. Before you begin, you may want to review book chapters 10–12 in *How (Not) to Read the Bible*.

> When we open the Bible to any section, we are also opening up the worldview of the original recipients, a way of seeing the world that is very different than our own.

1. Read "Ancient Israelite Bible Study Methods 101" on pages 164–175 in *How (Not) To Read The Bible* and briefly summarize your answers to the questions found in this section.

   Who were the original readers of Genesis?

Why was Genesis written and what did God want the original audience to know?

How did the audience understand the world around them?

2. Many questions arise when we try to analyze the Genesis creation story through the lenses of physics, astronomy, and modern botany. It's difficult to piece together various scenarios to explain how all of this could have happened—how the Earth maintained orbit without the gravitational pull of the sun; how light, morning, and evening all existed before the sun; and how light was commingled then separated from darkness if darkness is the absence of light. All of this can be so confusing!

But we miss the point of what God was communicating when we try to read these verses like an engineer or a scientist. Remember, the Israelites were wondering if God was more powerful than other gods. God wanted the Israelites to understand that he created it all, he had power over it all, and that the existence of other powerful things, such as the sun and moon—thought to be gods in ancient Egypt—were part of God's creation, not their own.

Six Days of Creation

How does God's creation of humans in his image reinforce the point God was communicating to the Israelites?

How is this different from the relationship between humans and other well-known gods in the ancient world?

3. Read Genesis 1:2. Imagine the earth as "formless and empty." This is a phrase in Hebrew that means *a desolate an uninhabitable wasteland.* Draw or describe the image that comes to your mind when you think of the earth this way.

Then read pages 191–193 in the book. *How does God bring order to chaos in the creation story?*

God's Work	Problem: Creation is "formless and empty" (1:2).	
	Forming	Filling
	Day 1: light and darkness	Day 4: the lights of day and night
	Day 2: sky and sea	Day 5: birds and fish
	Day 3: fertile earth	Day 6: land animals, including man
	Result: The work of creation is finished, and God can rest (2:1).	

What was God communicating through the symmetry found between Days 1–3 and Days 4–6 of the creation narrative? What does it mean for your life to see the way God operates with such purpose and intention?

4. Much mocking of the Bible is about a talking serpent and how God pulled a "rib" from the body of Adam and created Eve from this rib.

Read Genesis 2, particularly verses 20–22. What did these verses mean to their original recipients?

For more insight to your answer, read "The 'Rib-Woman' Was Not a Rib-Woman" on pages 204–206 in the book.

Now consider Genesis 3. What did these verses mean to their original recipients?

For more insight to your answer, read "How About That Talking Snake" on pages 206–209 in the book.

5. Read the seven interpretations of the six-day creation viewpoints in the book on pages 193–201. How would you summarize the viewpoint towards 1.) creation of the earth and 2.) creation of humans from each interpretation?

INTERPRETATION	CREATION OF EARTH	CREATION OF HUMANS
Young Earth		
Appearance of Age		
Gap		
Preparing the Garden & Promised Land		
Day-Age		
God's Temple		
Evolutionary Creation		

Recommended Resources for Further Study

Practical resources for making sense of the Bible-versus-Science conflict:

In the Beginning . . . We Misunderstood: Interpreting Genesis 1 in Its Original Context by Johnny Miller and John Soden (Grand Rapids: Kregel, 2012).

Biologos Foundation, *https://biologos.org*, founded by Francis Collins, an American physician-geneticist and lead on the Human Genome Project. BioLogos holds an evolutionary creationist viewpoint.

Reasons To Believe - https://reasons.org an old earth viewpoint.

Answers in Genesis: https://answersingenesis.org/ This is the
young earth viewpoint.

*Genesis Unbound: A Provocative New Look at the Creation
Account* by John Sailhaimer (Portland, OR: Dawson
Media, 2011).

*If you're interested in understanding the cosmic
worldview of the ancient Israelites, check out:*

*The Lost World of Genesis One: Ancient Cosmology and
the Origins Debate* by John Walton (Downers Grove:
InterVarsity, 2009).

"Genesis & Ancient Cosmic Geography" post by Tim Mackie
& Aeron Sullivan of The Bible Project, *https://bibleproject
.com/blog/genesis-ancient-cosmic-geography*.

*The Unseen Realm: Recovering the Supernatural Worldview
of the Bible* (Bellingham, WA: Lexham, 2015); and the
"Ancient Israelite Cosmology" video, both by Dr. Michael
Heiser, *https://drmsh.com/cool-motion-animation-video-of
-ancient-israelite-cosmology*.

For Next Week: Before your group's next session, read chapters
13–15 in *How (Not) to Read the Bible*.

My God Can Beat Up Your God

Does Christianity Claim All Other Religions Are Wrong?

> *"I am the way and the truth and the life."*
> JOHN 14:6 NIV

Welcome

Christianity often gets a bad rap for being "intolerant" by believing that Jesus is the only true path to God. Saying there is only one path to God, as the Bible so clearly states, feels wrong and divisive today. Especially when the idea that "all roads lead to God" is the most popular metaphor used to connect various religious perspectives under the banner of God as *love*. Like this:

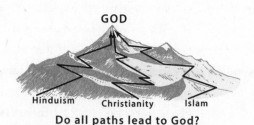

Do all paths lead to God?

This attractive and popular belief is the reason why we hear quotes from famous people who seem to lovingly care about people and don't want to promote "intolerant" ideas that lead to fighting and division. Saying all paths lead to the same God sounds wonderful, and I agree that if this metaphor were accurate, it would diminish much of the tension and awkwardness we find in talking about the differences between religions. But when we begin to ask questions about the various "paths" or religious perspectives, we start to see a clear fact emerge: *not all paths end up in the same place.* The "God" of each world religion is not the same God of the Christian faith, the God who sent his son Jesus as the only way back to himself. But this faith claim sounds intolerant to those who don't realize the paths are not the same—to those who haven't taken the time to explore and see that the paths are actually contradictory to each other.

Many gods

The triune God

The one God of the Qur'an

Hinduism   Christianity   Islam

... the paths lead to entirely different mountaintops

As a curious college student, the more I studied what Jesus said and taught, I realized it wasn't intolerant to believe Jesus as the only way to God—it was actually consistent with the rest of the Bible story. It was also consistent with the idea that God loves us so much that he sent Jesus to save and ransom us— just like a loving father would. Reading the "intolerant" verses in the context of a bigger storyline changed them from words of intolerance to words of love, from something disturbing to something beautiful. My life changed forever as I realized the truth and came to believe in Jesus as the way, the truth, and the life. And that is my hope for you, too. Let's take a closer look at the claims of the Christian faith in comparison to the claims of other religions.

Watch

Play the video segment for session five (see the streaming video access provided on the inside front cover). As you watch, use the following outline to record any thoughts or concepts that stand out to you.

Video Notes:

One Way to God:

> "Jesus answered, 'I am the way and the truth and the life. No one comes to the Father except through me. If you really know me, you will know my Father as well. From now on, you do know him and have seen him.'"
>
> *John 14:6–7 NIV*

> "For there is one God and one mediator between God and mankind, the man Christ Jesus, who gave himself as a ransom for all people. This has now been witnessed to at the proper time."
>
> *1 Timothy 2:5–6 NIV*

> "Salvation is found in no one else, for there is no other name under heaven given to mankind by which we must be saved."
>
> *Acts 4:12 NIV*

"Whoever has the Son has life; whoever does not have the Son
of God does not have life."

1 John 5:12 NIV

KEY QUESTION: Is Jesus the only way to God?

The Quest for truth about Jesus:

Making sense of popular ideas and common themes of today:

"I do believe that all paths lead to God. It's a shame that we end
up having religious wars because so many of the messages are
the same."

—MADONNA

"There are many paths, many ways to what you call God. There couldn't possibly be one way."

—OPRAH WINFREY

The Golden Rule

". . . do to others what you would have them do to you . . ."

Matthew 7:12 NIV

Buddhism: "Treat not others in ways you yourself would find hurtful"

(Udana Varga 5:18)

Islam: "Not one of you truly believes until you wish for others what you wish for yourself"

The Prophet Muhammad; Hadith

Hinduism: "This is the sum of duty; do not do to others what would cause pain if done to you"

Mahabharata 5:151

(Read page 246 in the book for more examples)

ALL PATHS LEAD TO GOD: is this true?

The backstory of the Bible: the idea of **one God.**

"In the beginning God created the heavens and the earth."

Genesis 1:1 NIV

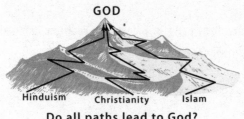

GOD

Hinduism Christianity Islam

Do all paths lead to God?

"For there is one God . . . "

1 Timothy 2:5 NIV

"There had been a primitive monotheism before men and women started to worship a number of gods. In the beginning, therefore, there was one God."

—KAREN ARMSTRONG, *A HISTORY OF GOD*

Bible Storyline

Humans rebel against God

Sin enters the world and causes the loss of God's presence and corruption.

God promised redemption through Jesus

"And I will put enmity between you and the woman, and between your offspring and hers; he will crush your head, and you will strike his heel."

Genesis 3:15 NIV

Prophecies about Jesus:
- be born of a virgin (Isaiah 7:14)
- be born in Bethlehem (Micah 5:2)
- take on people's sin and bring healing by his death (Isaiah 53:4–5)

"But he was pierced for our transgressions, he was crushed for our iniquities; the punishment that brought us peace was on him, and by his wounds we are healed."

Isaiah 53:5 NIV

The Life and Death of Jesus:

"Yet it was the Lord's will to crush him and cause him to suffer,
   and though the Lord makes his life an offering for sin,
   he will see his offspring and prolong his days,
   and the will of the Lord will prosper in his hand . . .
   because he poured out his life unto death . . .
   For he bore the sin of many . . . "

Isaiah 53:10, 12 NIV

"For there is one God and one mediator between God and mankind, the man Christ Jesus, who gave himself as a ransom for all people."

1 Timothy 2:5–6 NIV

"Salvation is found in no one else, for there is no other name under heaven given to mankind by which we must be saved."

Acts 4:12 NIV

All of these prophecies about Jesus came true.

The church was born. The good news of Jesus was spreading.

The true original story of one God, one Savior: *Jesus as the bridge between God and humans.*

KEY QUESTION: But don't all paths lead to God?

There is a very common assumption that all paths lead to God. So different religions such as Hinduism, Islam and Christianity may look different, but all end up at the same place.

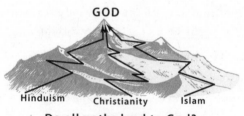

Do all paths lead to God?

But when you look at each world religion, you see that they have extremely different beliefs about God, salvation, the afterlife, who Jesus is etc.

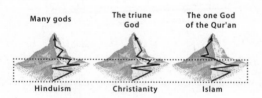

**. . . the paths lead to entirely
different mountaintops**

The problem is that when you look at a base level, there often is some teachings that are similar like the Golden Rule (treat your neighbor as yourself). There is truth and some good teaching in all world religions.

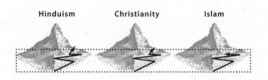

At the base level there is common truth among faiths

However, when you study further and examine the fuller beliefs about each faith you discover they are extremely different with beliefs and the paths end up at entirely different mountaintops.

. . . the paths lead to entirely different mountaintops

They don't all end up in the same place.

The Bottom Line: *either one is right and the rest are wrong, OR they're all wrong and something else is right.*

This is why we need to then have confidence that the Scriptures are from God and true. Which then shows Christianity's validity and truth.

The reality: Jesus is the only way and one path to God. There aren't many paths.

TOUGH QUESTION: What about those who never hear about Jesus but live a faithful life?

> "For since the creation of the world God's invisible qualities—his eternal power and divine nature—have been clearly seen, being understood from what has been made, so that people are without excuse."
>
> *Romans 1:20 NIV*

God is love.

CONCLUSION: it's our job as Christians to tell others about Jesus as the way, the truth, and the life. It is not unloving or divisive to believe that something is true. It is unloving not to share the truth with others about Jesus being the way of salvation.

> "The Lord is not slow in keeping his promise, as some understand slowness. Instead he is patient with you, not wanting anyone to perish, but everyone to come to repentance."*
>
> *2 Peter 3:9 NIV*

> *repentance: to change your direction in the right way*

Believing Jesus as the only way leads to forgiveness, salvation, and eternal life in God.

Group Discussion:

Take a few minutes with your group members to discuss what you just watched and explore these concepts in Scripture.

1. What stood out to you from listening to Dan today? What insights or remaining questions do you have about Jesus as the only way to God?

2. As Dan mentions, have you ever considered or heard from others that Jesus as the only way to God according to Scripture is *arrogant, unloving, and divisive?* Why or why not?

3. Role-play and have someone make the claim that all paths lead to God. Have someone else draw the series of mountain diagrams to show and explain how when examined deeper, that doesn't make sense and all paths don't lead to the same mountaintop (see diagrams above in the Video Notes).

4. Read Romans 1:20–23. Paul tells the Romans that they are without excuse for believing in God. What kind of examples does he give of people who refuse to believe? How do we see these examples play out in our lives today?

5. Read John 14:1–14. Here we find Jesus with his disciples on the eve of his death. Thomas asks Jesus about physical directions for finding Jesus, and Jesus responds with an answer about spiritual identity. How did this moment redefine our understanding of Jesus?

6. What does it mean to you for Jesus to be the one true way to God? How does this belief impact your everyday actions and conversations? What are you doing to tell the world around you about Jesus?

Reflection

Briefly reflect on the teaching and any notes you took. In the space below, write down your most significant takeaway from this session. Also, consider what discussion question or Bible passage you're going to explore as a result of today's session. If time permits, share it with your group.

Wrap-Up

Pray as a group before you close your time together. If you're already a Christian, ask God to help you tell other people about the uniqueness of Jesus as the way, the truth, and the life. Thank God for the courage he's already given you to live as though this is really true (*because we believe it is true*) and pray that each of you would continue to grow in the grace and knowledge of Jesus. And if you're still exploring Christianity, ask God to give you the vision to see the truth about Jesus and the Bible beyond those crazy-sounding verses.

How You Can Respond

Choose at least one of the following suggested activities/reflections to complete over the next week. Consider sharing with your friends or small group members the impact the activity or reflection had on you as you spent this time exploring. Before you begin, you may want to review book chapters 13–15 in *How (Not) to Read the Bible*.

> I don't believe all paths lead to God. I am convinced that what Jesus said is true, so I want to spend my life doing whatever is possible to see others come to know Jesus as the way, the truth, the life, and the way to God.

1. On page 217 in the book, Dan outlines a list of common emotions we might feel and questions we might ask if we're still questioning Jesus as the only way to God. Read that section and identify which emotion or question has resonated most with you, either right now or in the past. Write it down here. Also, use this space to write down any other emotion or question you've experienced around this topic.

The emotion or question that resonated with you:

How did Dan's teaching help you clarify how you think and feel about Jesus as the only way to God?

2. Read pages 222 and 228–229 in the book (and bonus if you reread Genesis 1–3). According to Dan, why does the Bible begin with the idea of one God who created all things? Why is this significant to our understanding of Jesus as the only way to God?

In the beginning
(Genesis 1–2)

harmony with
God and
each other

3. At a time when people were spreading across the globe with new languages and beliefs, the people of Israel began compiling their inspired writings into what we call the Hebrew Bible or the Old Testament. Most of the prophets spoke and wrote their inspired words between 1000 to 400 B.C., the same time new religions and faiths were developing. The prophecies about Jesus in the Old Testament are significant to our understanding of Jesus as the only way to God. Read these passages and make note of what each prophecy has to say about the future "messiah" who will "save the world":

Isaiah 7:13–17:

Micah 5:1–9:

Isaiah 53:

Then consider: What does it mean to you to realize that God had a long-term plan lasting thousands of years to save the world from the consequences of human evil—a plan that included a way for us to know him and be forgiven by him through the sacrifice of Jesus?

4. Read "Key Verses That Indicate There Is One God and Only One Way" on pages 233–236 in the book. What stands out to you about these verses, individually and collectively, and Jesus' claim to be "the way"? How do each of these passages characterize Jesus?

John 14:6

Acts 4:12

1 Timothy 2:5–6

John 3:16–18 (added here)

5. Christianity often gets a bad rap for being intolerant and claiming to have the one true path to God in Jesus. But if you look further into most other world faiths, you will find the same thing: beliefs and claims regarding the "right way." The main world religions share a few basic things in common, but they diverge in clear and distinct ways as they move deeper into their beliefs and practices.

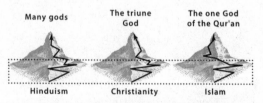

When you go beyond a base level see where the paths keep going to . . .

Read pages 240–243 in the book to take a look at these differing beliefs and practices, particularly the core questions of
*Who is God? Who is Jesus? and How do we attain salvation in
the afterlife?* Summarize the answers using your own words.

Christianity:

Hinduism:

Islam:

The biggest difference here? *Jesus.* Each one of these questions and the various answers is crucial to our understanding
of the one true faith. However, the most important piece to
seeing the Christian faith as the one true way is Jesus' to be
truth itself. This is what sets Jesus apart from Hindu Vedas,
Muhammed, and Buddha, and every other leader claiming to
possess the truth and the way. How is Jesus—as the way, the
truth, and the life of our salvation—the full expression of God's
love for us? How do you know God's love to be true for you?

Recommended Resources for Further Study

Practical resources for making sense of
Jesus as the one true way to God:

Encountering World Religions: A Christian Introduction by
    Irving Hexham

The Compact Guide To World Religions by Dean Halverson

If you're interested in hearing a pop culture
perspective on "intolerant" Christian faith:

"*Oprah—One Way Only?*" YouTube, *https://www.youtube.com
    /watch?v=cOxmd3cpxgY.*

For Next Week: Before your group's next session, read chapters
16–18 in *How (Not) to Read the Bible.*

Rated NC-17

The Horror of Old
Testament Violence

> *You will keep in perfect peace those whose minds are steadfast, because they trust in you.*
>
> ISAIAH 26:3 NIV

Welcome

In this session we're talking about an extremely difficult topic: *violence in the Old Testament.* This topic is difficult not because it's hard to find examples (I wish this were the case), but because it's hard to address. Many people still believe the Bible is a book filled with good stories and happy things we can teach to our children, which is still true. But I'm frequently surprised by the number of people who are naively unaware of the violence contained in Scripture, whether or not they grew up in a Christian home. If we take a closer look, stories taught in traditional Sunday School or classrooms, such as Noah's Ark or Joshua and the Battle of Jericho, have been sanitized to skip the violent parts. But the internet and social media sites are now flooded with memes and graphics that call out the violent reality behind so many classic stories, and we can no longer skim over the violence.

It's easy to make generalizations and level accusations against the God of the Bible when we read a violent passage without the full context of the Bible's storyline. Many of the violent acts in the Bible are the result of evil human choices and decisions. So, just because something evil is mentioned

in Scripture, doesn't mean that God approves of those actions and behaviors. As I hope to show today, there are legitimate reasons as to why we see violence in the Bible. I also hope to dispel some of the misunderstandings and criticisms surrounding this violence as it relates to our perspective of God. We will see how applying basic Bible study methods to the troubling passages about violence shows us there is more happening in the story, much more than we would be aware of in a brief surface-level reading of just a few verses. Using our analogy of the Bible as a library, we can see that most of the violence in the Bible library is located in the "history books" section.

While some of us may have used this idea of biblical violence as a way to distance ourselves from God, for me, digging deeper into studying these verses has given me a deeper understanding of God's great love, patience, forgiveness, and compassion. The fact that God didn't inspire the writers to "clean up" or "filter out" human evil actually makes me trust the Bible more, knowing the difficult parts were not edited out. Instead of pushing me away from the God of the Bible, this understanding has strengthened my faith and love in God. And I hope the same can be true for you after our teaching today.

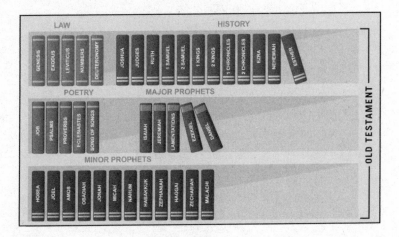

Watch

Play the video segment for session six (see the streaming video access provided on the inside front cover). As you watch, use the following outline to record any thoughts or concepts that stand out to you.

Video Notes:

Violence in the Bible: there are no simple answers!

Noah's Ark

Joshua and the Battle of Jericho

> When the trumpets sounded, the army shouted, and at the sound of the trumpet, when the men gave a loud shout, the wall collapsed; so everyone charged straight in, and they took

the city. They devoted the city to the LORD and destroyed with the sword every living thing in it—men and women, young and old, cattle, sheep and donkeys.

Joshua 6:20–21 NIV

"This is what the Lord Almighty says: . . . Now go, attack the Amalekites and totally destroy all that belongs to them. Do not spare them; put to death men and women, children and infants, cattle and sheep, camels and donkeys.'"

1 Samuel 15:2–3 NIV

Happy is the one who seizes your infants
and dashes them against the rocks.

Psalm 137:9 NIV

New Testament Jesus vs. Old Testament God

Three ways to view violence in the Bible:

1. The "no apology" approach

   The problem with this approach:

2. The "Bible is wrong" approach

   Marcion (140 AD): different God in the Old Testament vs. New Testament

Old Testament God	New Testament Jesus

"Kill them" (Num. 25:16) "Show them no mercy" (Deut. 7:2)	"Love them" (Matt. 22:39) "Forgive them" (Luke 23:34)

The problem with this approach:

3. The "understand the whole Bible storyline to know God's character" approach

   YouTube video: "Scary Mary" (look up "Scary Mary" on YouTube to see the actual video)

The problem of not using this approach:

IF GOD WAS ON TWITTER:

"The Lord, the Lord, the compassionate and gracious God, slow to anger, abounding in love and faithfulness, maintaining love to thousands, and forgiving wickedness, rebellion and sin."

EXODUS 34:6–7 NIV

KEY QUESTIONS: What about the violent Bible verses?

Three key ways to understand violence in the Bible:

1. Humans in the Bible chose violent bloody acts on their own (Psalm 137:9).

   ASK: Is it humans doing the violence or God command-ing the violence?

   Most of the violent verses about God (sending Israel into battles) are from a *lim-ited* time period in biblical history, and these battles were not genocide. It was about God *driving out,* not *wiping out* (Deuteronomy 11:16; 12:31–32).

   ASK: Is this about God making way for his presence, or is it hyperbole of the day?

> *Hyperbole* means exaggerated statements or claims not meant to be taken literally.

2. God always gave warnings of death or destruction over hundreds of years (2 Chronicles 33, Ezekiel 18:23 and 33:11,16, 2 Peter 3:9).

   ASK: What kind of warning has God given, and what kind of patience has God exhibited?

3. Death is the reality of wars and battles.

   KEY QUESTION: Can we trust who God is and why death happened under his care?

   "The Lord, the Lord, the compassionate and gracious God, slow to anger, abounding in love and faithfulness, maintaining love to thousands, and forgiving wickedness, rebellion and sin."

   Exodus 34:6–7 NIV

> When we understand the God of the whole Bible, we then trust in his character and his compassion and understand he is a loving and forgiving God.

God's compassion towards you is the gift of Jesus.

Group Discussion:

Take a few minutes with your group members to discuss what you just watched and explore these concepts in Scripture.

1. What stood out to you from listening to Dan today? Which one of the three approaches to explaining violence in the Bible is most familiar to you?

2. Read the following illustrations of violence in the Bible: Psalm 137:7–9 (human violence), Deuteronomy 11:13–17 (God *driving out*, not *wiping out*), and Ezekial 18:21–23 (God's warning). How does this insight change your view of violence in the Bible?

3. Dan mentioned the hyperbole and rhetoric used by biblical authors to write about the death and destruction they were causing and experiencing. Can you think of examples today of how we might use this kind of language, too (*i.e. sports, video games, etc.*)?

4. Read the story of King Manasseh in 2 Kings 21:1–18. How are all three examples of violence illustrated here in one passage? How do we make sense of this violence?

5. Read the story of Nineveh in Jonah 3. Why was God planning to destroy Nineveh? What made God change his mind?

6. As Dan mentions, we can trust God and his compassion despite the violence we read about in the Old Testament, and we never have anything to fear with God because of the sacrifice of Jesus (John 3:16–17). Do you believe this is true for you? Why or why not?

Reflection

Briefly reflect on the teaching and any notes you took. In the space below, write down your most significant takeaway from this session. Also, consider what discussion question or Bible passage you're going to explore as a result of today's session. If time permits, share it with your group.

Wrap-Up

Pray as a group before you close your time together. Ask God to give you the vision for the right approach to view the difficulties of violence in the Bible. Thank God for the compassionate ways he loved his people despite the disturbing ways they refused to accept God's love, and instead chose violence and punishment. And thank God for the ultimate sacrifice of Jesus who endured a violent death on the cross to make things right with God, so you can live in freedom with God rather than fear of God. Praise God for your personal experience of God's abundant love, immense kindness, and endless forgiveness.

How You Can Respond

Choose at least one of the following suggested activities/reflections to complete over the next week. Consider sharing with your friends or small group members the impact the activity or reflection had on you as you spent this time exploring. Before you begin, you may want to review book chapters 16–18 in *How (Not) to Read the Bible.*

> When I struggle with violence in the Bible, I try to recall the God of the whole Bible—the God who is patient, loving, compassionate, and forgiving. And I trust that although there are mysteries I may not know in this life, I have more than enough truth from Scripture to keep faith and trust in God. I may not understand why violence happened, but I trust the God who does.

1. Read 1 Chronicles 13 and Matthew 27:45–50, and "Ways to Explain the Violence in the Bible that Aren't Satisfying" on pages 264–267 in the book. It's easy to feel a little guilty when we raise questions that seem to doubt God's wisdom, such as *"Why is there violence in the Bible if God is a loving*

God?" But perhaps this isn't us doubting God's wisdom, rather it's *seeking* God's wisdom. God wants us to understand him by looking at his actions. God wants us to know him better by asking him why he does what he does. With this in mind, asking God *"Why?"* isn't a bad thing. We see several writers in the Bible doing the very same thing. Wondering *"Why?"* and trusting that there is a good reason is never seen by God as wrong or sinful.

Why does King David question God in this passage? What's going on in David's world?

How does God indirectly show David he can still trust God (vs.14)?

Jesus asked the ultimate "Why, God?" question on the cross. Notice how he didn't question all of the violence heaped upon him, he questioned God's presence. How has the violence in the world caused you to question God's presence?

In what other ways are you asking "Why, God?" about something difficult today?

2. Since the time of Jesus, the historical church has believed that we must accept God for who he is, and this understanding of him is preserved for us in the Bible—the entire Bible. This means, we don't get to choose the parts of it we like, and we don't get to shape God into the God we prefer him to be. The fact that Jesus believed the entire Old Testament as God's inspired word is a major reason we can accept the battle-filled, violent stories in the history books of the Old Testament. Jesus really believed what Moses and the rest of the prophets wrote, and he never once alluded to any part of the Old Testament not being accurate or true. So it was never the God of the Old Testament vs. the Jesus of the New Testament, as critics may claim. In fact, Jesus often quoted the Old Testament, emphasizing the importance of its truth.

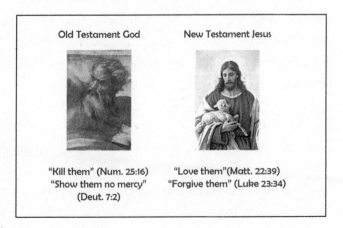

Old Testament God

New Testament Jesus

"Kill them" (Num. 25:16)
"Show them no mercy"
(Deut. 7:2)

"Love them"(Matt. 22:39)
"Forgive them" (Luke 23:34)

Here are two examples of Jesus using the Old Testament to explain his actions:

- Why his ministry fulfilled the OT prophecies: Matthew 13:14–15, Mark 4:12, Luke 8:10, and Isaiah 6:9–10
- Why he rebuked the Pharisees and Scribes for their lip service to God: Matthew 15:8–9, Mark 7:6–7, and Isaiah 29:13

What stands out to you about these examples?

What changes for you when you see how Jesus believed the truth of the entire Old Testament—violence and all?

For more examples of why and when Jesus quoted Old Testament prophets, read "Postlude: Jesus Loved His Crazy Bible" on pages 293–298. You can also do an extended search online using this key phrase: "Jesus quoting the Old Testament."

3. Read The Parable of the Net (Matthew 13:47–52), and the story of Ananias and Sapphira (Acts 5:1–11). When you study the New Testament books of the Bible, you quickly see that talk of violence and judgment didn't end with the Old Testament. But you will also see how the way God relates to people changes after Jesus. God still exercises power and intervenes in ways that at times cause death (Ananias and Sapphira). But it is Jesus who talks most about judgment, specifically the judgment of *Hell*—otherwise known as the eternal fire and punishment for those who reject God. On several occasions, Jesus gives a stark warning to people who go against God's guidance, that they will end up in "Gehenna," the valley in south Jerusalem where piles of garbage, including animal carcasses and the dead bodies of people who didn't have families, burned daily. Jesus was making a graphic point that the spiritual decomposition of hell never ends. This was how he described the consequences of rejecting God, otherwise known as *sin*.

> It is better for you to enter the kingdom of God with one eye than to have two eyes and be thrown into hell, where "the worms that eat them do not die, and the fire is not quenched."
>
> *Mark 9:47–48 NIV*

Which refers to the Old Testament verse:

> "And they will go out and look on the dead bodies of those who rebelled against me; the worms that eat them will not die, the fire that burns them will not be quenched, and they will be loathsome to all mankind."
>
> *Isaiah 66:24 NIV*

For more, read "Jesus Spoke about Hell and Judgement More Than Anyone Else in the Bible" on pages 268–269 in the book. Then answer the following questions:

How do you make sense of these difficult passages about Hell, especially coming from Jesus?

Even though the New Testament didn't have bloody battles, it still reveals a holy God who hates sin (2 Thessalonians 1:7–9). How do you reconcile the idea of a loving God who hates sin?

4. Read Exodus 34. There are times in the Old Testament where God acts out of judgment that leads to death. And it's important to note that the people groups involved in that kind of harsh judgment were first warned, pleaded with to change, and shown great patience for a while before they experienced God's wrath. (And it's important to note that when God does express anger in the Old Testament, it's righteous anger to uphold justice and defend the innocent.) The story of Moses and the second set of Ten Commandments illustrates the great patience of God, even when death was deserved. Moses previously came down from the mountain and found the Israelites worshiping and honoring a false god (Exodus 32). But God gives them a second chance (along with many, many, many other second chances) because God wanted the people who just rejected him by worshiping another god to know that he is a loving God to his people.

"The LORD, the LORD, the compassionate and gracious
God, slow to anger, abounding in love and faithfulness,
maintaining love to thousands, and forgiving wickedness,
rebellion and sin."

Exodus 34:6–7 NIV

How has God been these things to you through the life of
Jesus (compassionate, gracious, slow to anger, abounding
in love, and faithful) even when you've rebelled or sinned
against God?

5. Read "Genocide and Mass Killing" on pages 275–288 in the
book. It's true there are a lot of battles and deaths throughout
the whole Bible, but not all were sanctioned or commanded
by God. When God sent Israel into battle with various cities
in the "promised land," his intention was not to destroy but
to drive out. And God always gave the people he was driving out the opportunity to avoid battle by turning towards
him. These people groups were given the opportunity to join
Israel in worshiping the one true God, or remain in rebellion
against God and be removed from God's land. It was about
occupation, not ethnicity or race. God was creating a physical
place where he could dwell with his people and restore the
community lost in the Garden of Eden. To do this, he needed
to remove those who worshiped other gods and engaged in
wicked, evil practices. If he didn't, evil would spread like
cancer to the Israelites, taking over their hearts and minds.

"Extermination"	"No Extermination"
Joshua 10:20a: "It came about when Joshua and the sons of Israel had finished slaying them with a very great slaughter until they were destroyed."	Joshua 10:20b "and the survivors who remained of them had entered the fortified cities."
Joshua 10:39: "every person" in Debir was "utterly destroyed."	Joshua 11:21: Later Joshua "utterly destroyed" Anakites in Debir.
Joshua 11:21: The Anakites were "cut off" and "utterly destroyed" in Hebron—as well as from Debir, Anab, and "all the hill country of Judah." There were "no Anakim left in the land of the sons of Israel."	Joshua 15:13–14: Caleb "drove out" the Anakites from Hebron; cf. Judges 1:20, where Caleb "drove out" the Anakites from Hebron.
Judges 1:8: "Then the sons of Judah fought against Jerusalem and captured it and struck it with the edge of the sword and set the city on fire."	Judges 1:21: "But the sons of Benjamin did not drive out the Jebusites who lived in Jerusalem; so the Jebusites have lived with the sons of Benjamin in Jerusalem to this day."
Joshua: 11:23: "So Joshua took the whole land, according to all that the LORD had spoken to Moses, and Joshua gave it for an inheritance to Israel according to their divisions by their tribes. Thus the land had rest from war."	Judges 2:21, 23: "I also will no longer drive out before them any of the nations which Joshua left when he died. . . . So the LORD allowed those nations to remain, not driving them out quickly; and he did not give them into the hand of Joshua."

Paul Copan and Matthew Flannagan, *Did God Really Command Genocide? Coming to Terms with the Justice of God* (Grand Rapids: Baker, 2014).

So it's ironic when God is criticized for putting an end to evil practices among Old Testament people groups by punishing those who engaged and advocated for evil. Any hope for people to eventually be set free from their addiction to evil and their tendency to reject God's guidance (sin) lay in preserving Israel for God's future plans.

How were the battles of the Old Testament ultimately about the protection of Israel and the fulfillment of God's plans to save the world through Jesus?

Why do so many people today criticize God for not ending evil and suffering in the world? And how does this session help you make sense of an answer to this criticism?

What makes you willing to trust God—the God of the entire Bible—even when you have questions and when particular stories, such as the violence in the Old Testament, don't seem to make sense?

Recommended Resources for Further Study

Practical resources for making sense of violence in the Bible:

Philosophia Christ 11, "We Don't Hate Sin So We Don't Understand What Happened to the Canaanites," no. 1 (2009): 01.

Did God Really Command Genocide? Coming to Terms with the Justice of God by Paul Copan and Matthew Flannagan (Grand Rapids: Baker, 2014).

Jonah, Nahum, Habakkuk, Zephaniah, The NIV Application
   Commentary (Grand Rapids: Zondervan, 2004).
   A critic's view of violence in the Bible:
Drunk with Blood: God's Killings in the Bible by Steve Wells
   (Lahore, Pakistan: SAB, 2003).

Closing Words

> "A Bible that is falling apart usually belongs to someone who isn't."
> —CHARLES SPURGEON

As we end this study, I do hope that whether you are a
Christian or not—that this experience has brought you some confidence knowing there are ways to respond to the difficult parts
of the Bible. For those who are Christians, I don't think we have
the choice to *not* be in the Bible regularly in today's world because
there are so many discussions and opinions out there about God,
theology, and Jesus. If we're not regularly in the Bible, then it's
hard to determine what's true and what isn't. Anyone can take a
verse or two or three and form a belief from it about something
they want to believe, but that's not how to read the Bible. When
we do make Bible reading and study a consistent part of our lives,
it is less likely we then go down a misleading path. If we study
these difficult passages, we will also be better prepared when
we hear or read criticisms of the Bible, we can then help others
when questions come up.

Above all, I hope this study draws you closer to God. The
more we read and study the Bible, the more our hearts will
expand in love for him as we get to know him more. The more

we read and study the Scriptures, the more we will read about his consistent love and compassion for us.

Thank you for going through this study and please feel free to contact me with any other questions or stories of how the study went for you.

—*Dan Kimball, www.dankimball.com*

Leader's Guide

Thank you for your willingness to lead your group through this study. What you have chosen to do is valuable and will make a great difference in the lives of others. The rewards of being a leader are different from those of participating, and we hope that as you lead you will find your own walk with Jesus deepened by the experience.

How (Not) To Read the Bible is a six-session Bible study built around video content and small-group interaction. As the group leader, imagine yourself as the host of a dinner party. Your job is to take care of your guests by managing the behind-the-scenes details so that as your guests arrive, they can focus on one another and on the interaction around the topic for that week.

As the group leader, your role is not to answer all the questions or reteach the content—the video, book, and study guide will do most of that work. Your job is to guide the experience and cultivate your small group into a connected and engaged community. This will make it a place for members to process, question, and reflect—not receive more instruction.

There are several elements in this leader's guide that will help you as you structure your study and reflection time, so be sure to follow along and take advantage of each one.

Before You Begin

Before your first meeting, make sure the group members have a copy of this study guide. Alternately, you can hand out the study guides at your first meeting and give the group members some time to look over the material and ask any preliminary questions. Also make sure they are aware that they have access to the videos at any time through the streaming code provided on the inside front cover. During your first meeting, send a sheet of paper around the room and have the members write down their name, phone number, and email address so you can keep in touch with them during the week.

Generally, the ideal size for a group is eight to ten people, which will ensure that everyone has enough time to participate in discussions. If you have more people, you might want to break up the main group into smaller subgroups. Encourage those who show up at the first meeting to commit to attending the duration of the study, as this will help the group members get to know one another, create stability for the group, and help you as the leader know how to best prepare each week.

Each of the sessions begins with an opening reflection. The questions that follow in the "Share" section serve as an icebreaker to get the group members thinking about the general topic at hand.

Some people may want to tell a long story in response to one of these questions, but the goal is to keep the answers brief. Ideally, you want everyone in the group to get a chance to answer, so try to keep the responses to a minute or less. If you have talkative group members, say up front that everyone needs to limit their answer to one minute.

Give the group members a chance to answer, but tell them to feel free to pass if they wish. With the rest of the study, it's generally not a good idea to have everyone answer every question

—a free-flowing discussion is more desirable. But with the opening icebreaker-type questions, you can go around the circle. Encourage shy people to share, but don't force them.

At your first meeting, let the group members know each session contains a personal study section that they can use to reflect more on the content during the week. While this is an optional exercise, it will help the members cement the concepts presented during the group study time and encourage them to spend time each day in God's Word. Let them know that if they choose to do so, they can watch the video for the following week by accessing the streaming code found on the inside front cover of their studies. Invite them to bring any questions and insights they uncovered while reading to your next meeting, especially if they had a breakthrough moment or didn't understand something.

Weekly Preparation

As the leader, there are a few things you should do to prepare for each meeting:

- Read through the session. This will help you to become more familiar with the content and know how to structure the discussion times.
- Decide how the videos will be used. Determine whether you want the members to watch the videos ahead of time (via the streaming access code found on the inside front cover) or together as a group.
- Decide which questions you want to discuss. Based on the amount and length of group discussion, you may not be able to get through all the questions, so choose four to five that you definitely want to cover.

- Be familiar with the questions you want to discuss. When the group meets, you'll be watching the clock, so you want to make sure you are familiar with the questions you have selected. In this way, you'll ensure you have the material more deeply in your mind than your group members.
- Pray for your group. Pray for your group members throughout the week and ask God to lead them as they study his Word.
- In many cases, there will be no one "right" answer to the question. Answers will vary, especially when the group members are being asked to share their personal experiences.

Structuring the Discussion Time

You will need to determine with your group how long you want to meet each week so you can plan your time accordingly. Generally, most groups like to meet for either ninety minutes or two hours, so you could use one of the following schedules:

SECTION	90 MINUTES	120 MINUTES
Welcome (members arrive and get settled)	10 minutes	15 minutes
Share (discuss one or more of the opening questions for the session)	15 minutes	20 minutes
Watch (watch the teaching material together and take notes)	25 minutes	25 minutes
Discuss (discuss the Group Discussion questions you selected ahead of time)	30 minutes	45 minutes
Respond/Pray (reflect on the message, pray together as a group, and dismiss)	10 minutes	15 minutes

As the group leader, it is up to you to keep track of the time and keep things on schedule. You might want to set a timer for each segment so both you and the group members know when your time is up. (There are some good phone apps for timers that play a gentle chime or other pleasant sound instead of a disruptive noise.)

Don't be concerned if the group members are quiet or slow to share. People are often quiet when they are pulling together their ideas, and this might be a new experience for them. Just ask a question and let it hang in the air until someone shares. You can then say, "Thank you. What about others? What came to you when you watched that portion of the teaching?"

Group Dynamics

Leading a group through *How (Not) to Read the Bible* will prove to be highly rewarding both to you and your group members. But you still may encounter challenges along the way! Discussions can get off track. Group members may not be sensitive to the needs and ideas of others. Some might worry they will be expected to talk about matters that make them feel awkward. Others may express comments that result in disagreements. To help ease this strain on you and the group, consider the following ground rules:

When someone raises a question or comment that is off the main topic, suggest that you deal with it another time, or, if you feel led to go in that direction, let the group know you will be spending some time discussing it.

If someone asks a question that you don't know how to answer, admit it and move on. At your discretion, feel free to invite group members to comment on questions that call for personal experience.

If you find one or two people are dominating the discussion time, direct a few questions to others in the group. Outside the main group time, ask the more dominating members to help you draw out the quieter ones. Work to make them a part of the solution instead of part of the problem.

When a disagreement occurs, encourage the group members to process the matter in love. Encourage those on opposite sides to restate what they heard the other side say about the matter, and then invite each side to evaluate if that perception is accurate. Lead the group in examining other Scriptures related to the topic and look for common ground.

When any of these issues arise, encourage your group members to follow these words from the Bible: "Love one another" (John 13:34), "If it is possible, as far as it depends on you, live at peace with everyone" (Romans 12:18), "Whatever is true . . . noble . . . right . . . if anything is excellent or praiseworthy— think about such things" (Philippians 4:8), and "Be quick to listen, slow to speak and slow to become angry" (James 1:19). This will make your group time more rewarding and beneficial for everyone who attends.

Thank you again for your willingness to lead your group. May God reward your efforts and dedication, equip you to guide your group in the weeks ahead, and make your time together in *How (Not) to Read the Bible* fruitful as you pursue God's health and wholeness.

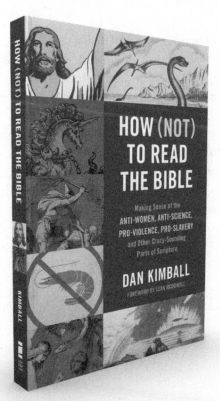

ReGENERATION
PROJECT

About the ReGeneration Project

If you are interested in joining with others who believe in the central importance of theology, apologetics, and the Bible to minister to new generations, please go to the ReGeneration Project website for more info.

We are a ministry of Western Seminary that is passionate about seeing younger generations become thinking Christians who love Jesus, Scripture, theology, and the church and desperately desire others to know Jesus too.

www.regenerationproject.org

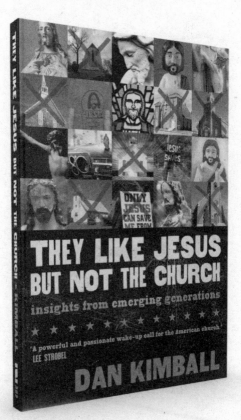

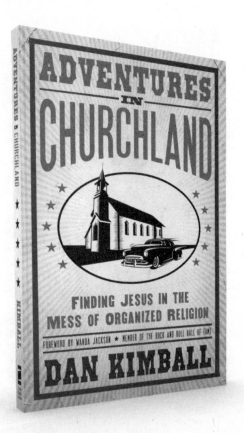